ANTHONY D'ATTILIO

SEASHORE LIFE
COLORING BOOK

DOVER PUBLICATIONS, INC., NEW YORK

PUBLISHER'S NOTE

This collection of more than 200 drawings by Anthony D'Attilio is an exciting introduction to the complex and fascinating field of plant and animal marine life. No matter which seashore you live near or visit on vacations, you will probably find some of its inhabitants represented in these pages.

Mr. D'Attilio prepared these drawings carefully and accurately, but in the interest of making the plates as decorative as possible he did allow himself some artistic license. Thus the specimens on any one plate are not necessarily to be found in the same body of water, and occasionally their relative sizes are not strictly correct.

You may be surprised, when you look at the covers of this book, by the wide range of colors and tones nature has subtly intermingled in her marine creatures. You can imitate this natural coloration, or you can use your imagination in selecting colors. The contour lines provided in the drawings can be used as guidelines for the subtle blending of colors, as in nature, or as sharp demarcation lines between areas of flat color, if your aim is more decorative. Whichever method you choose, enjoy coloring and creating for yourself either true-to-life depictions of marine plants and animals, or more fanciful creatures for framing or collages.

The varied specimens in this collection represent some of the most common and some of the most exotic forms of sea life in the oceans of the world. We hope these drawings and the identifications of the creatures will lead you to a deeper interest in this mysterious and still explorable area. You may then want to consult the more detailed field guides to marine life in your own area.

DOVER *Pictorial Archive* SERIES

This book belongs to the Dover Pictorial Archive Series. You may use the designs and illustrations for graphics and crafts applications, free and without special permission, provided that you include no more than four in the same publication or project. (For permission for additional use, please write to Dover Publications, Inc., 31 East 2nd Street, Mineola, N.Y. 11501.)

However, republication or reproduction of any illustration by any other graphic service whether it be in a book or in any other design resource is strictly prohibited.

International Standard Book Number: 0-486-22930-0

Manufactured in the United States of America
Dover Publications, Inc.
31 East 2nd Street
Mineola, N.Y. 11501

1. Clown anemone fish   2. Orange anemone   3. Wentletrap
4. Sea biscuit urchin

1

2

1. Berry seaweed   2. Feather star   3. Chiton   4. Limpets
5. Stony coral

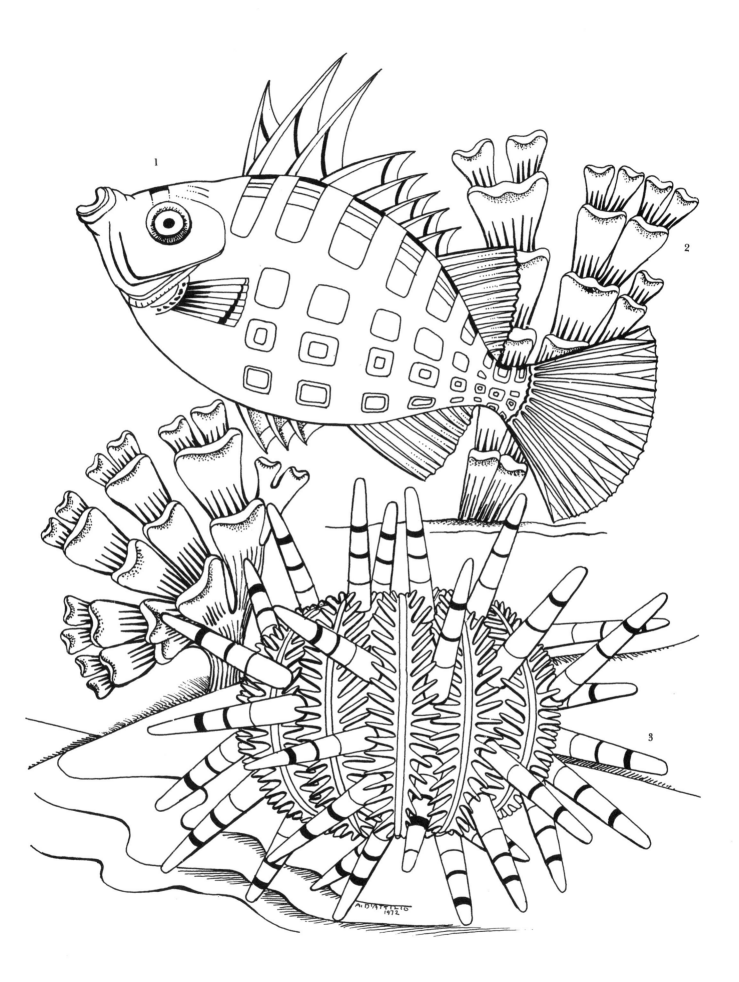

1. Porgy   2. Coral algae   3. Club-spined sea urchin

3

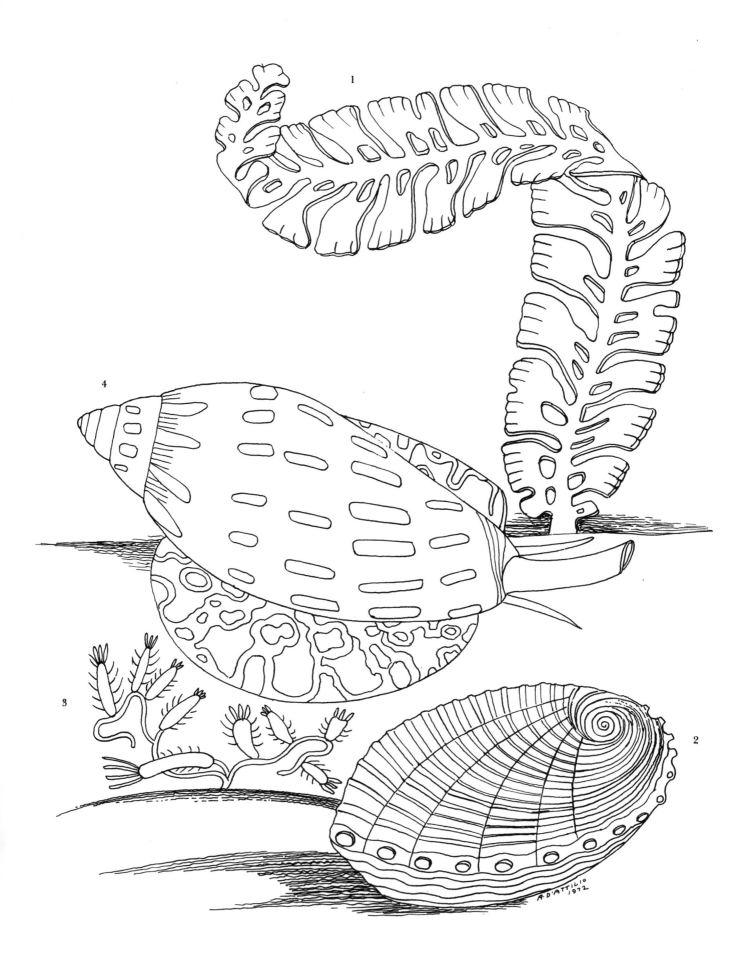

1. Kelp   2. Abalone shell   3. Branching crest animal
4. Volute

1. Tulip shell with Hermit crab   2. Branching hydrocoral
3. Keyhole urchin

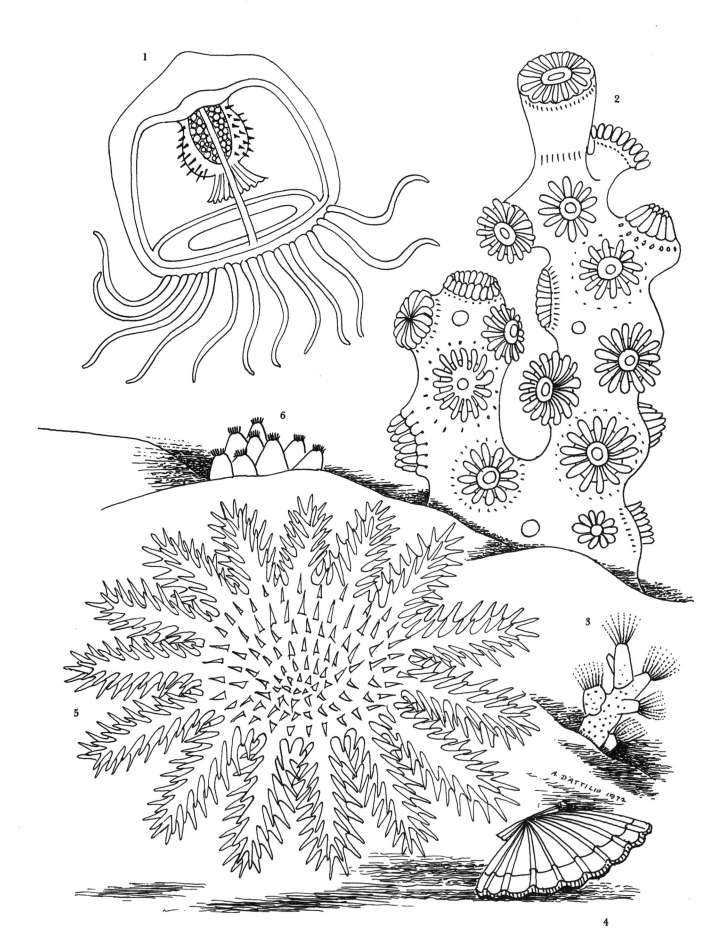

1. Hydromedusan jellyfish   2. Eyed coral   3. Sponge
4. Scallop   5. Spiny starfish   6. Sea squirts

1. Sea slug   2. Red seaweed   3. Sessile jellyfish
4. Scorpion fish   5. Alaria seaweed

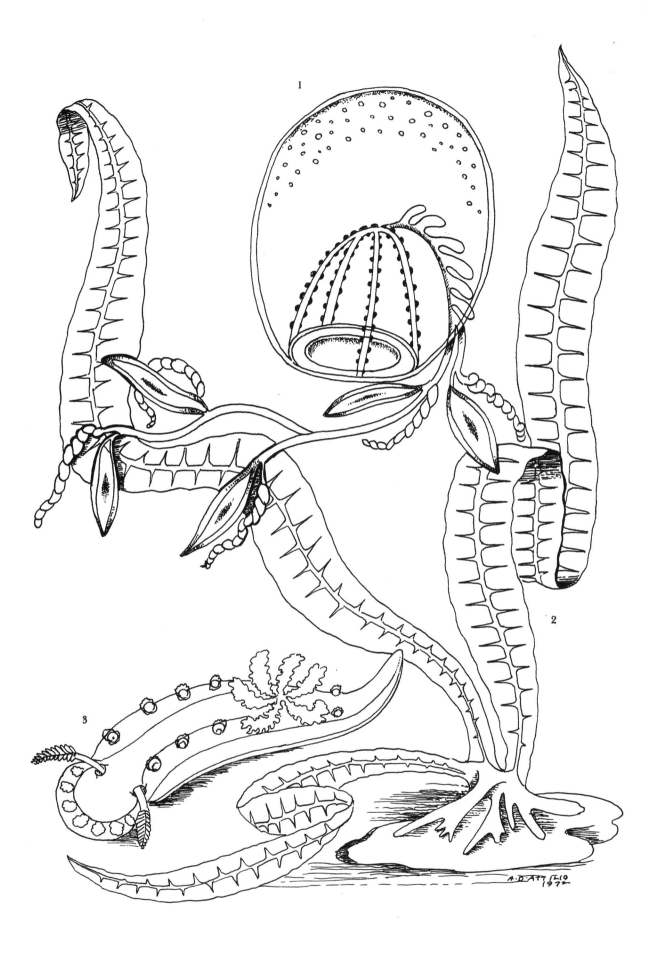

1. Bladder jellyfish   2. Kelp   3. Sea slug

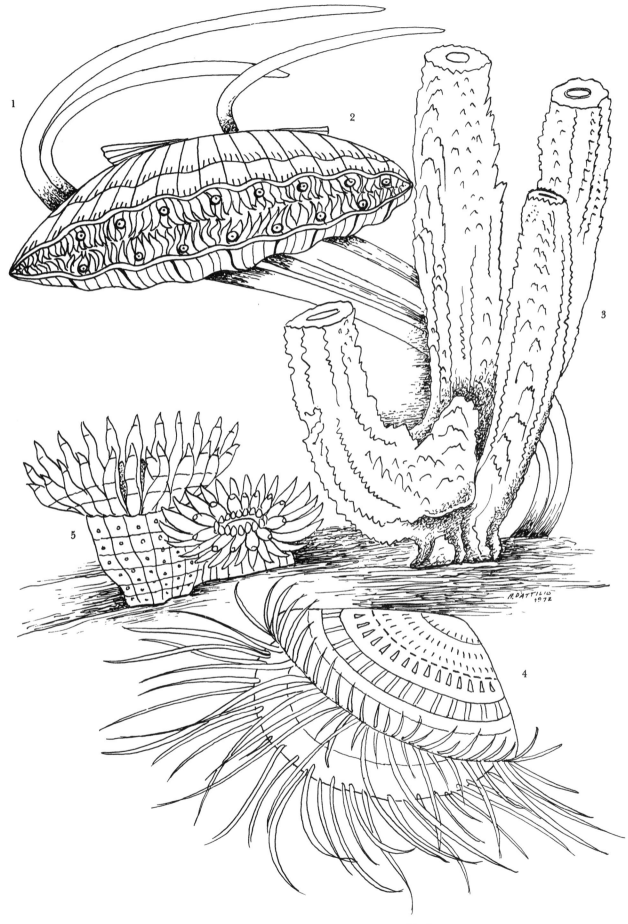

1. Sea grass   2. Scallop   3. Vase sponge   4. Lima bivalve
5. Blue anemone

9

1. Ivory shell   2. Sponge   3. Volva   4. Seaweed
5. Murex shell

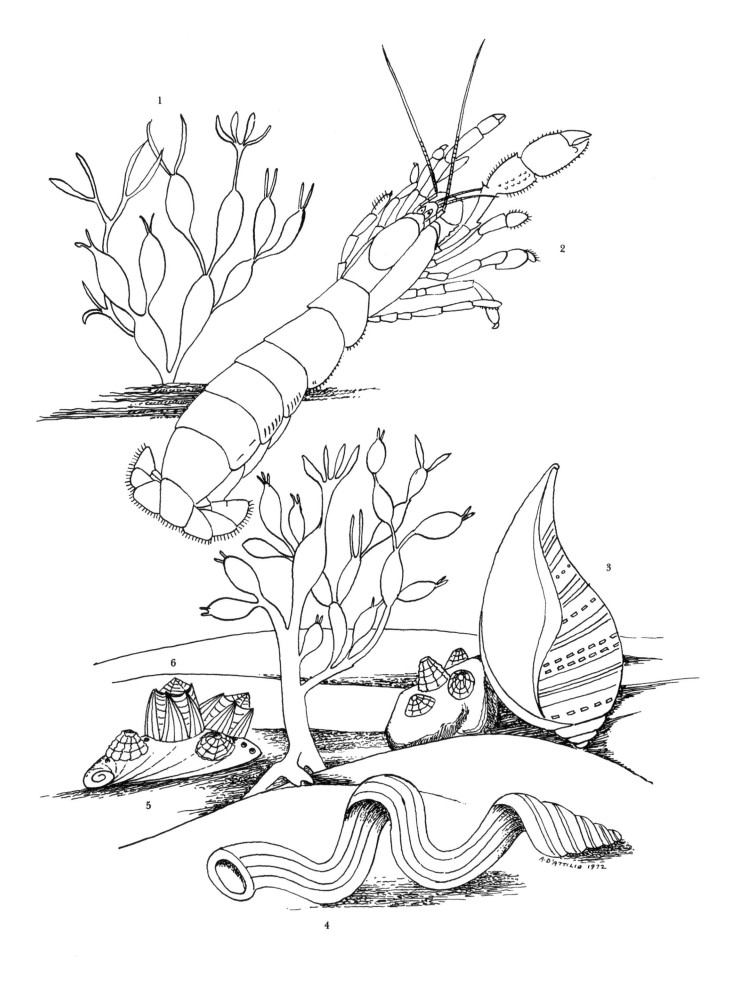

1. Brown blister weed   2. Ghost shrimp   3. Fig shell
4. Fargo's worm shell   5. Abalone shell   6. Rock barnacles

1. Oval ring weed   2: Sea squirts   3. Denuded sea urchin

1. Bubble shell   2. Saddleback butterfly fish
3. Clustering anemone   4. Gemmed anemone

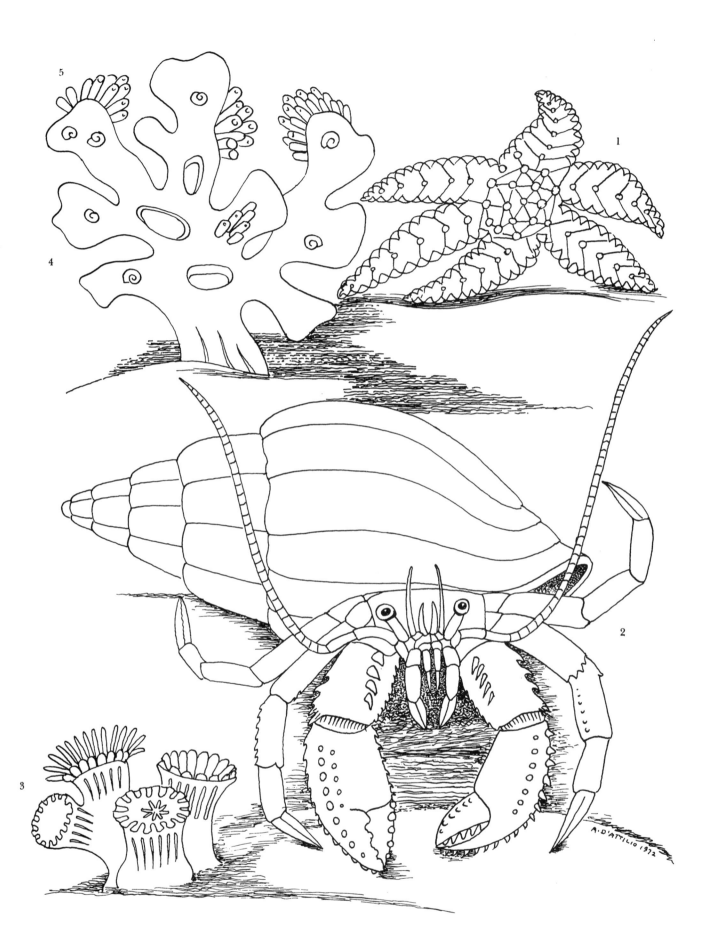

1. Common sea star   2. Hermit crab inhabiting Gastropod shell
3. Astrangia coral   4. Irish moss
5. Egg cases of shell animals

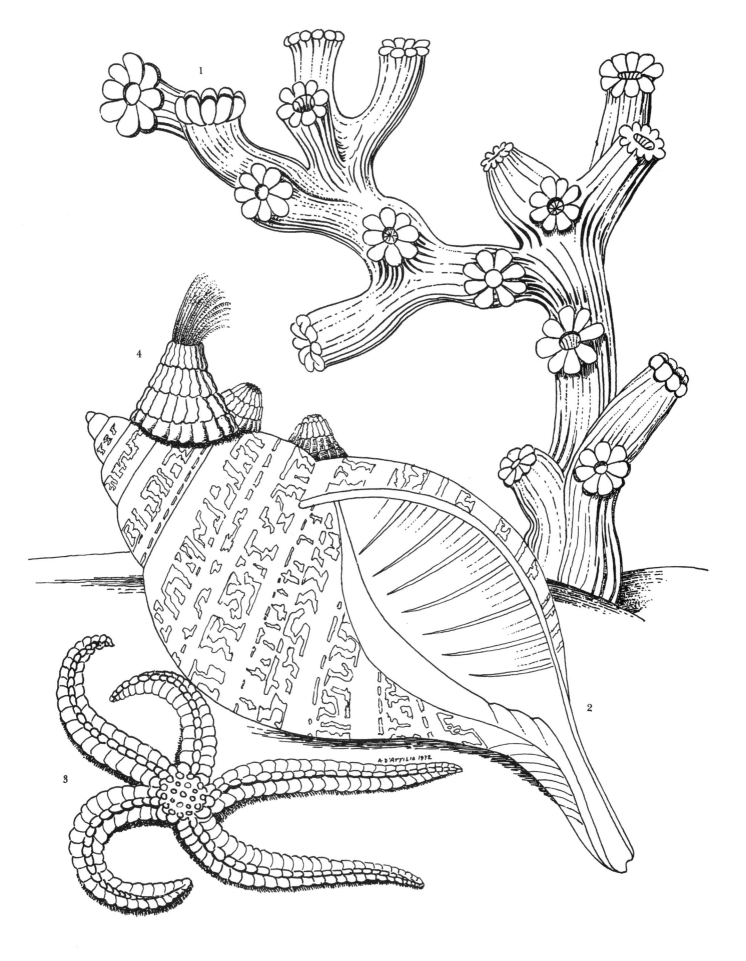

1. Branching coral   2. Tulip shell   3. Long-armed starfish
4. Rock barnacles

1. Triggerfish 2. Green soft coral 3. Bread-crumb sponge
4. Astrangia coral

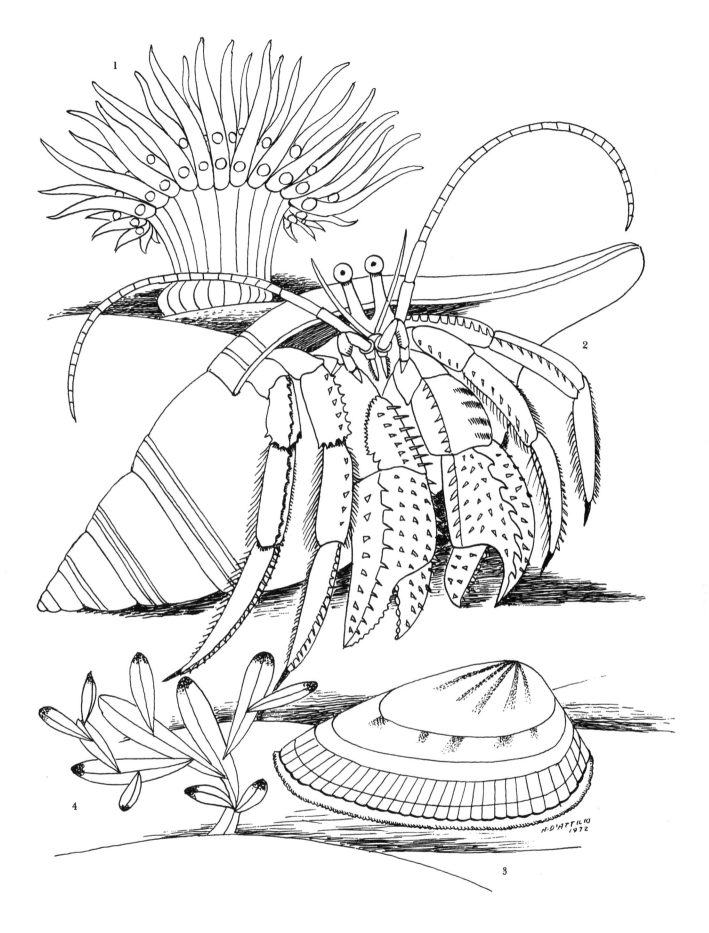

1. Sagartia anemone
2. Soldier hermit crab inhabiting Gastropod shell
3. Venus bivalve   4. Club seaweed

17

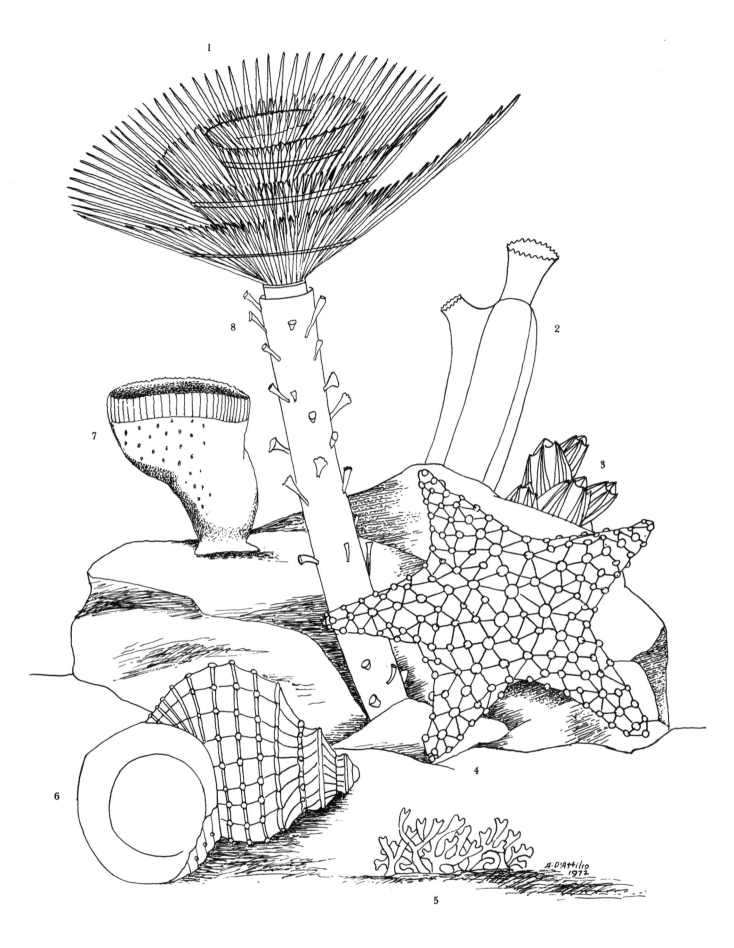

1. Fan worm in tube   2. Sea squirt   3. Rock barnacles
4. Ochre sea star   5. Seaweed   6. Turbo shell
7. Cup sponge   8. Hydroids

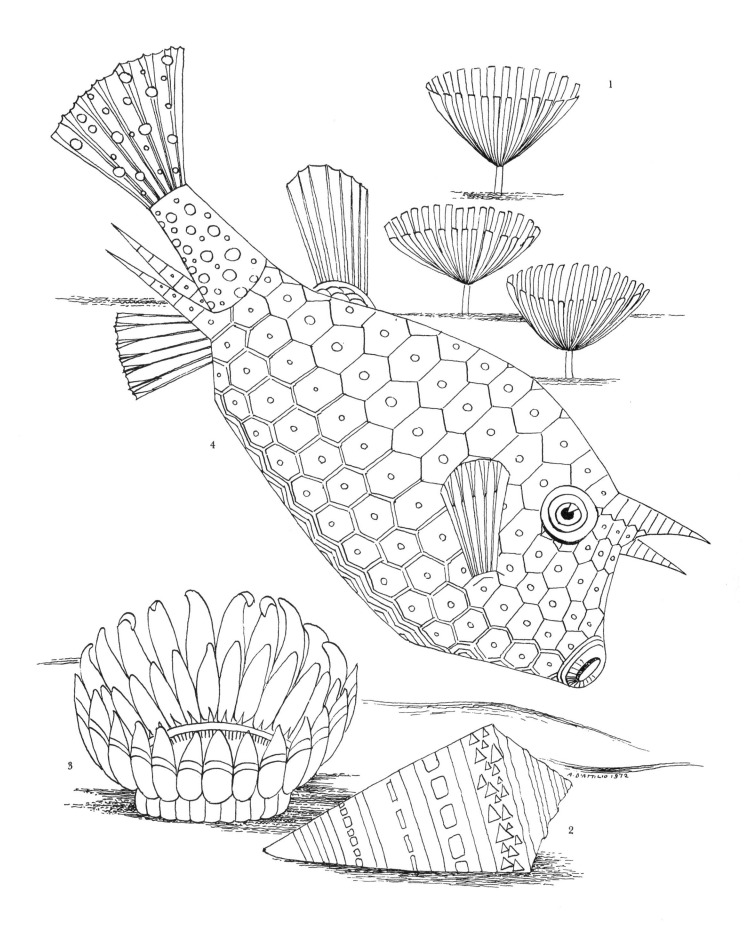

1. Sea daisies   2. Cone shell   3. Dahlia anemone
4. Cowfish

1. Long-nosed butterfly fish   2. Fan seaweed
3. Livona shell   4. Sea star

1. Surgeonfish   2. Codium seaweed   3. Soft coral
4. Coned sponges

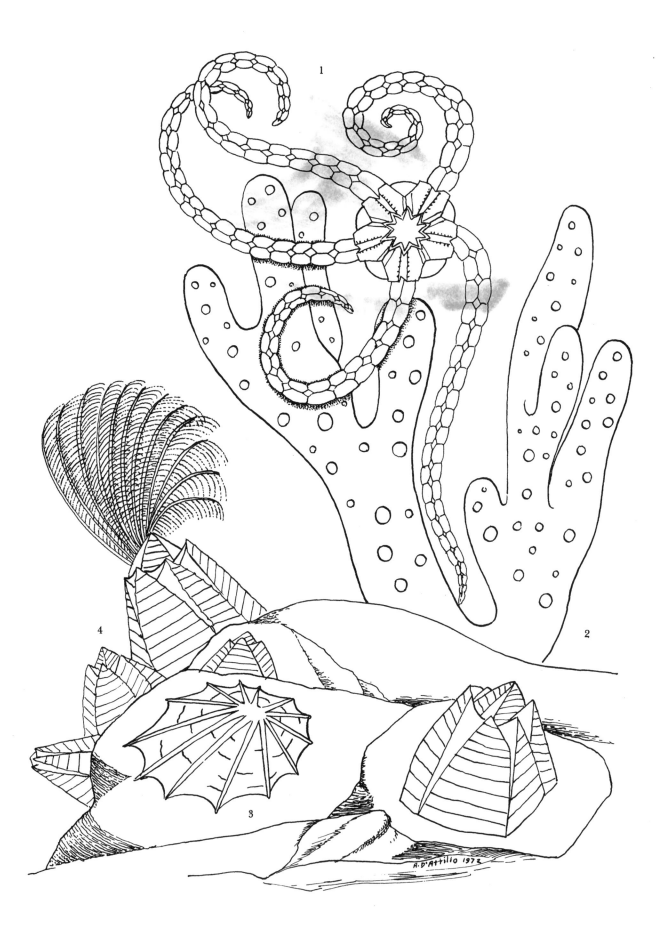

1. Brittle sea star 2. Branching hydrocoral 3. Limpet
4. Rock barnacles

1. Green branching fan weed   2. Stony algae   3. Scallop
4. Spiny lobster

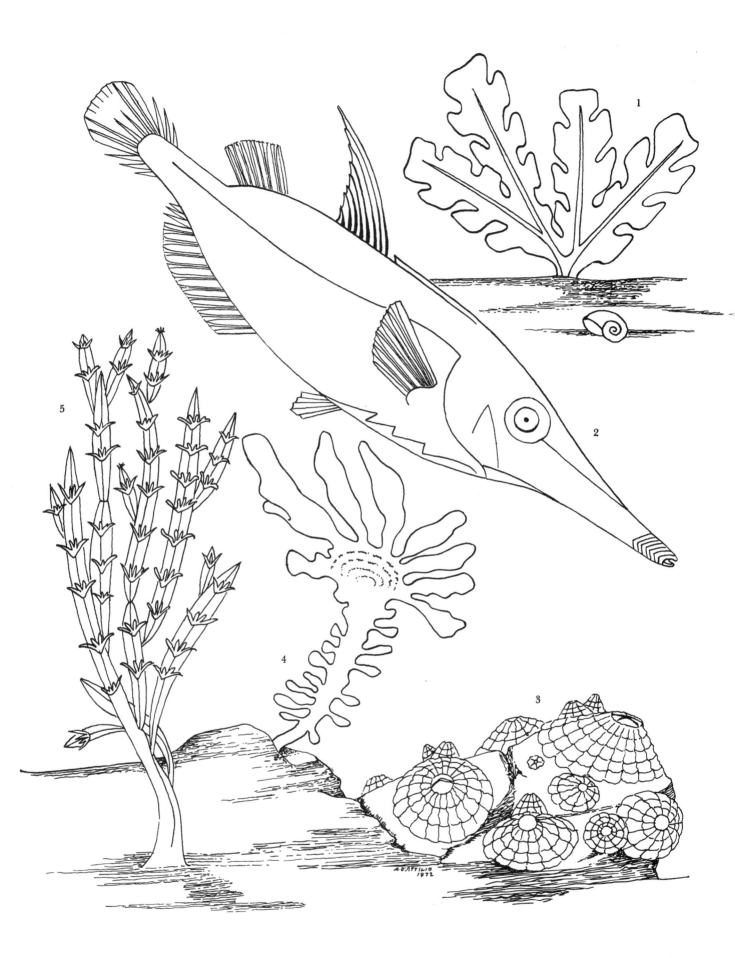

1. Palm seaweed   2. Long-nosed snook   3. Rock barnacles
4. Rocky pool green weed   5. Sea whip

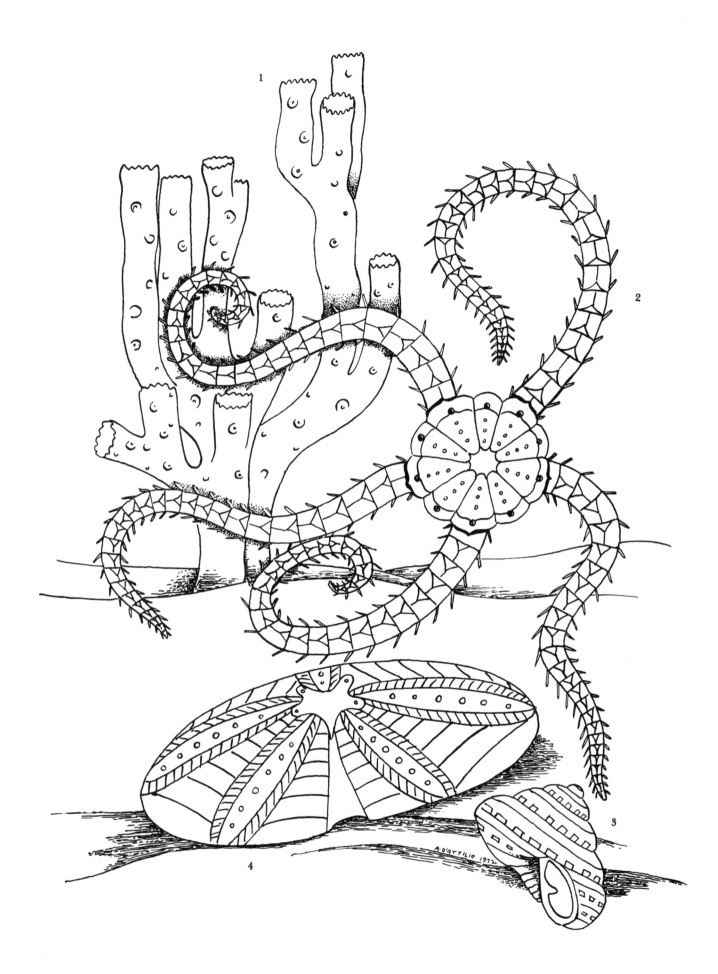

1. Branching sponge   2. Brittle sea star   3. Turbo shell
4. Sand dollar

1. Fringed Australian reef sea horse   2. Spotted snail
3. Burrowing shrimp   4. Brain coral

1. Mussels   2. Black-tip orange seaweed   3. Limpet
4. Plumed sea slug   5. Cancer crab   6. Goose barnacle

1. Leaflike flatworm 2. Common Easter sea star
3. Tellina shell 4. Gigartina seaweed

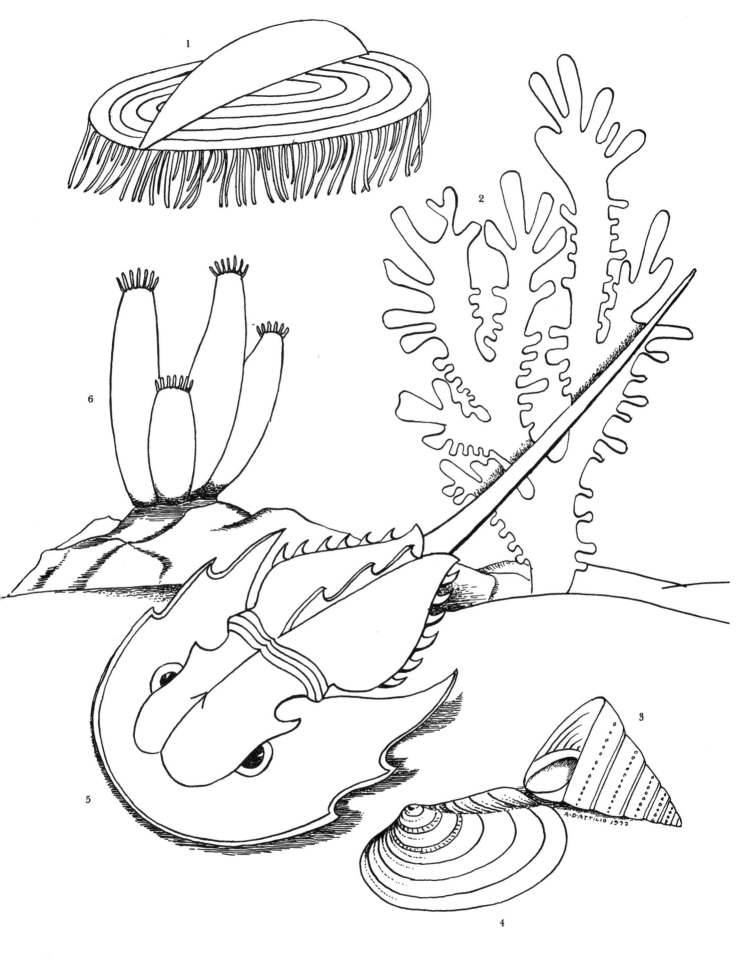

1. Vellela jellyfish   2. Alaria seaweed   3. Trochid shell
4. Bivalve shell   5. Horseshoe crab   6. Lime sponge

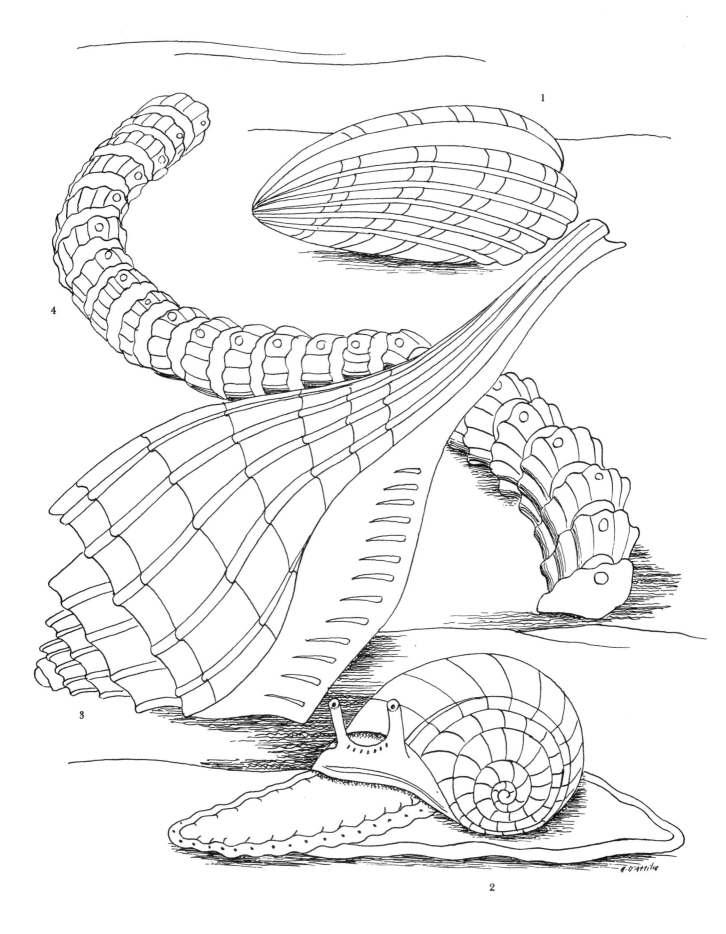

1. Mussel   2. Shark-eye Polynices shell   3. Whelk
4. Whelk egg case

1. Japanese sea horse   2. Staghorn coral   3. Sponge
4. Short-legged crab

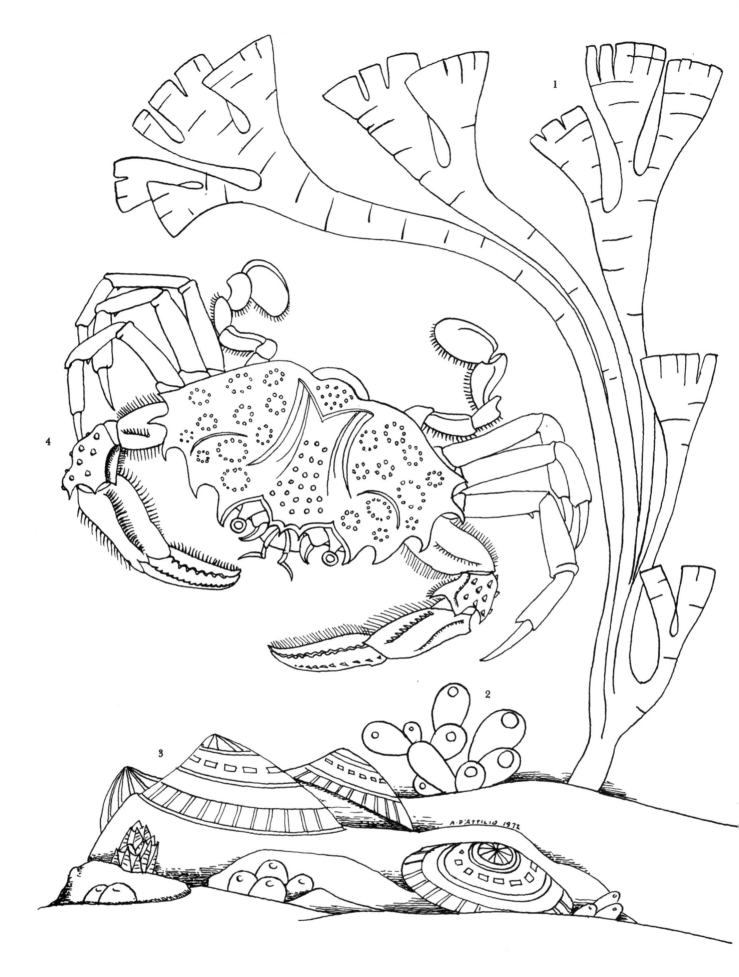

1. Purple fantip seaweed   2. Yellow sponge   3. Limpet
4. Calico crab

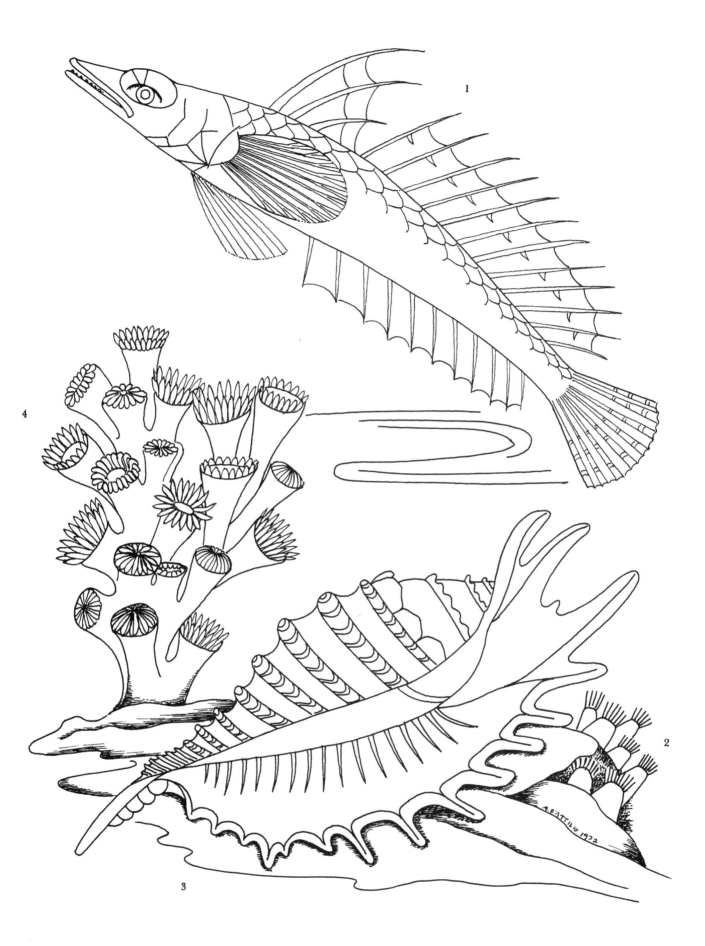

1. Spiny sea fish   2. Sponges   3. Violet scorpion shell
4. Astrangia coral

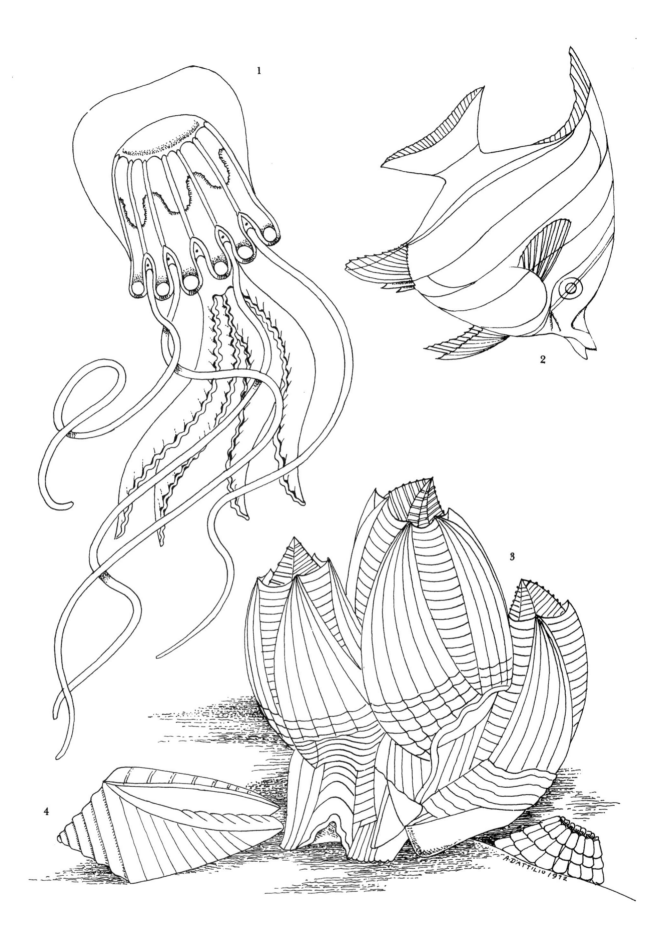

1. Jellyfish   2. Angelfish   3. Rock barnacles
4. Cone shell

1. Goby   2. Kelp   3. Rock barnacles   4. Pheasant shell
5. Swimming crab   6. Blenny

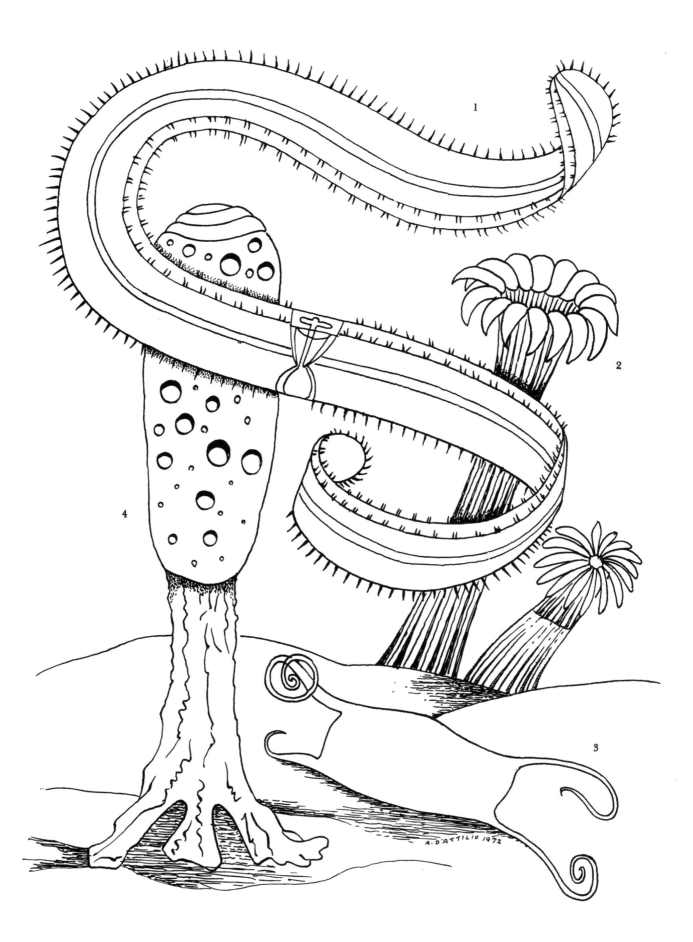

1. Comb jellyfish   2. Zooanthid anemone
3. Sea skate egg case (Sea purse)   4. Column sponge

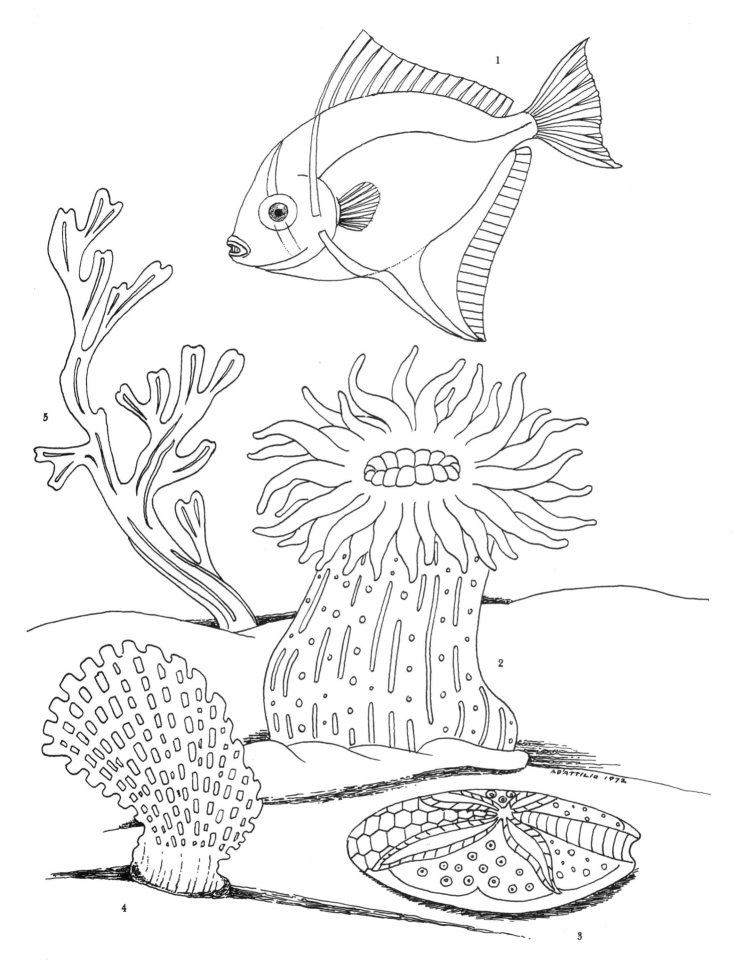

1. Moonfish   2. Orange anemone   3. Sand dollar
4. Purple sea fan   5. Green seaweed

1. Atlantic sea horses   2. Sea grass

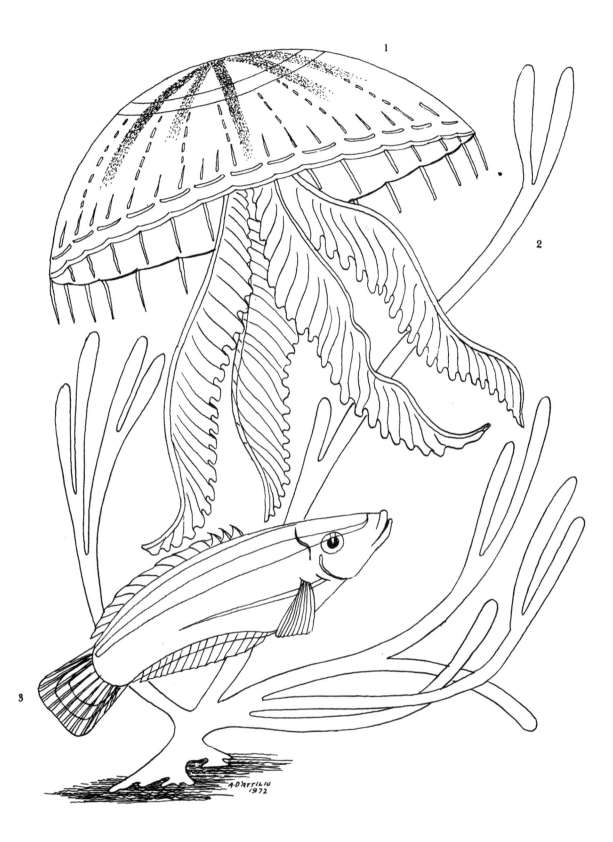

1. Moon jellyfish   2. Sea whip   3. Emperor fish

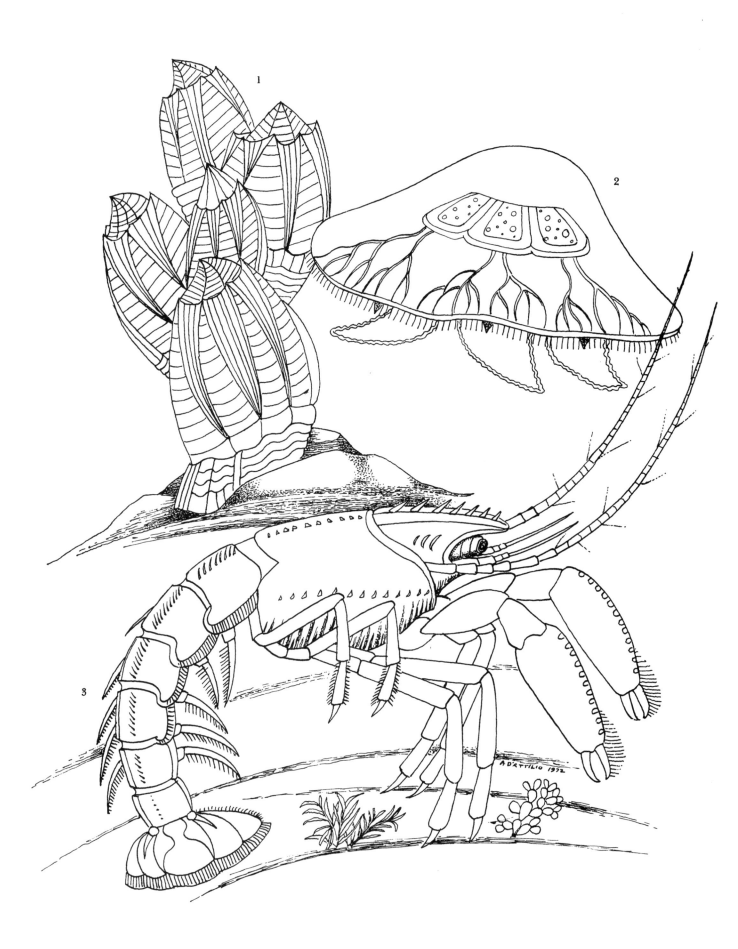

1. Rock barnacles   2. Aurelia jellyfish   3. Prawn

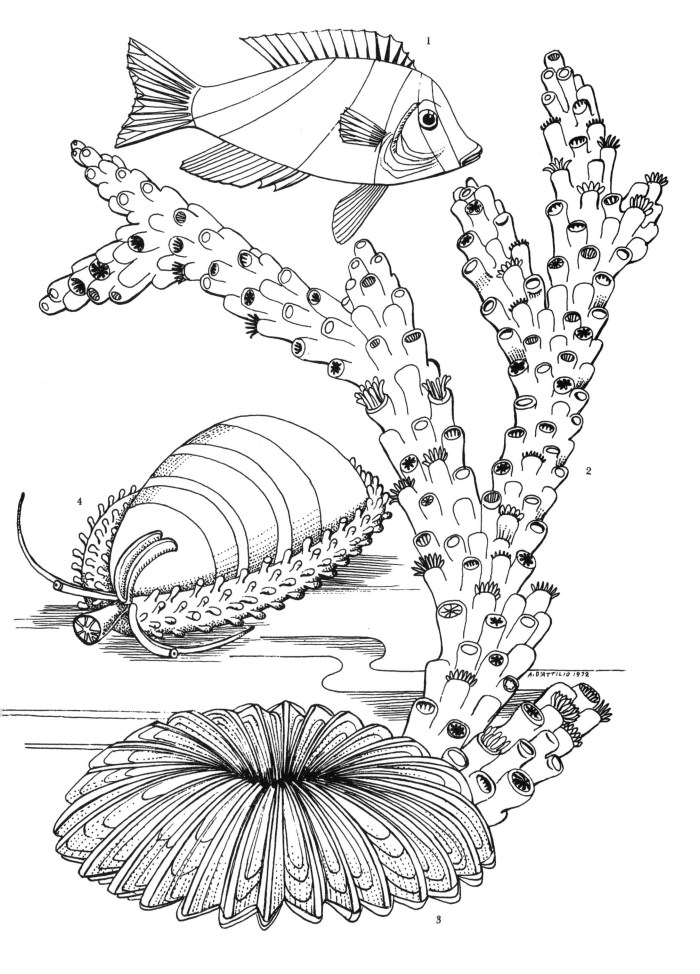

1. Snapper   2. Staghorn coral
3. Stony mushroom coral   4. Cowry

1. Small rock cod   2. Dead man's fingers sponge
3. Spotted siphonalia   4. Stony branching coral
5. Sundial shell

1. Mediterranean cuttlefish   2. Stony algae
3. Strombus shell   4. Mexican chiton   5. Rock barnacles

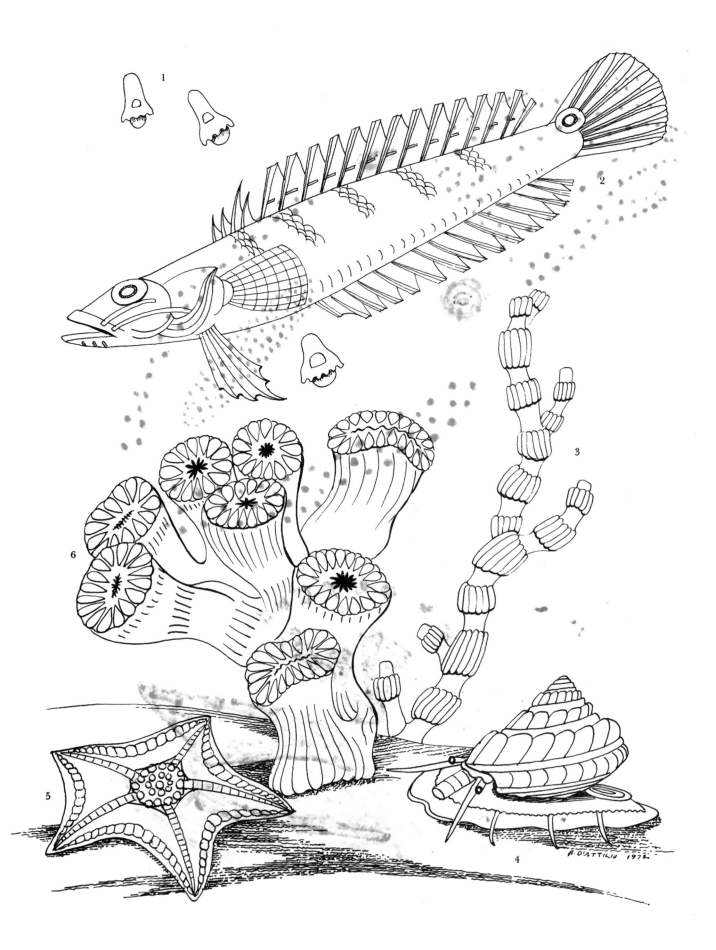

1. Hydroids   2. Wrasse   3. Coralline   **4. Top shell**
5. **Blue sea star**   6. Madreporarian orange reef coral

1. Red seaweed   2. Harp shell   3. Blue and green coral
4. West Australian volute

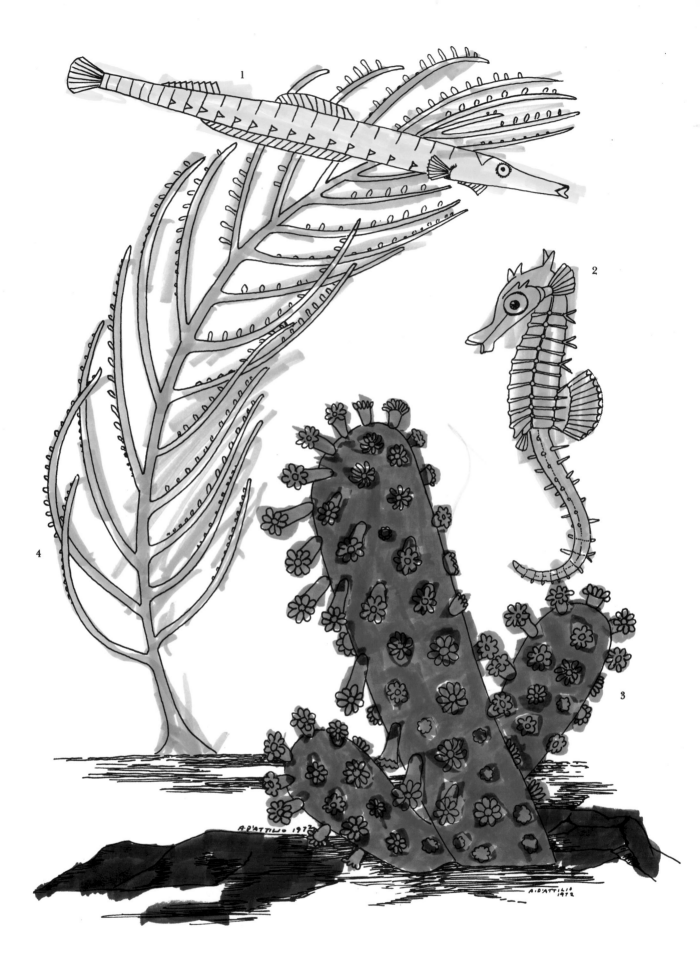

1. Pipefish   2. Young sea horse
3. Blue coral showing polyps   4. Sea whip